SMALL PLATES

Chris Cambell (he/they) is a nonbinary, Native American immigrant with ADHD. He writes poetry for performance and publication. His work examines the stories society overlooks, highlights the inequality that this demonstrates, and explores how we can use our creativity to break this cycle. Chris is a slam champion, has been published in anthologies internationally, and has competed in the UK National Poetry Slam finals twice, so far.

Jem Henderson (they/them) is a genderqueer poet from Leeds, winner of a Creative Future award for underrepresented writers. *genderfux*, their first collaboration came out February 2022. *an othered mother*, their first pamphlet, is out now from Nine Pens.

Praise for *Small Plates*

Small Plates by Chris Cambell and Jem Henderson is a humorous and forward-thinking pamphlet from two poets, one whom describes himself as 'non-binary' the other who describes themself as 'Gender Queer'. The poems flow in a stream of consciousness style with a pleasantly daft understanding of reality. 'is that it?' ask the two poets in the standout poem 'Like Your Last Dollars Week After Payday'. In the immortal words of Julian Casablancas: This is it

— Charlie Baylis, *a fondness for the colour green*

Cambell and Henderson cook up a sumptuous tasting menu of a collaboration worthy of recognition by Michelin… All flavours of the human experience are present and in expert balance, served in refreshing and vibrant ways throughout. Just delicious.

— Rick Dove, *Supervillain Origin Story*

A rich, sensual, and heartbreaking exploration of how tangible the poverty gap is. Immaculately considered and assembled with all the precision and intricacy of a five star meal. The juxtaposition will leave you spellbound and melancholy in equal turns.

— King Stammers

This innovative collection is as lovingly crafted as the dishes described! *Small Plates* had me feeling invested, protective, claustrophobic and free all at the same time. The Cyclical Natures of Sestina and Trauma is an unsettling masterpiece. They never let you stop long enough to process the trauma alongside the poets. Yet somehow Cambell and Henderson make you feel held and safe all the way through. Go eat with them. Order from the Small Plates section and don't let anyone else tell you when you're finished.

— Dee Dickens, *Fear of drowning*

Small Plates

Chris Cambell
&
Jem Henderson

Broken Sleep Books

ISBN: 978-1-915760-47-0

Cover designed by Aaron Kent

Edited & Typeset by Aaron Kent

Broken Sleep Books Ltd
Rhydwen
Talgarreg
Ceredigion
SA44 4HB

Broken Sleep Books Ltd
Fair View
St Georges Road
Cornwall
PL26 7YH

Contents

pre-dinner drinks

Apparently She Was Just Helping Us to Our Table   9

a simple welcome

A Simple Welcome   13

If That's Hello, Goodbye Might Kill Me   14

pebble

As if Our Teeth Weren't Broken Enough   17

My Poems Are Like Pebbles   18

washcloth

No One Said Magic Had to Be Useful   21

The Pill   22

lamb

Spirited Away // No-Face   27

Gush   29

ragstone

Ragstone   33

Something Taller Than Everest   34

rabbit

The Cyclical Nature of Sestina and Trauma   37

Why Wasn't This Served With Three Fingers of Laphroaig?   39

mussels

Mussels With Coal Oil   43

hake

John D. Rockefeller   49
I Drink at Least Two Litres of Water Every Day   50
On the Pinot   51

bbq

Jus the Colour of Canned Cranberries, My Only Food [...]   55
The Roast Beef of Old England   56

bathroom break

Like a Virgin   59

fondue

Fondue Four Nights a Week Without Cheese   63

rhubarb fool

Gretel   67
Rhubarb Fools   68

chocolate

Chocolate   71
Taste Buds Always Tell the Bitter Truth   72

cloud

Like Your Last Dollar a Week After Payday   77
You Don't Belong Here   78

pints in the pub after

Last Orders   81

Poem Authors   87
Acknowledgements   89

pre-dinner drinks

a flute of champagne

Apparently She Was Just Helping Us to Our Table

I can measure all the champagne
that's graced my lips in sips.
So when the server,

> *I think she's a server?*
> *Is that the right word?*
> *Wait, is she asking us to leave?*
> *But we had to pay in advance!*
> *NON-REFUNDABLE!*
> *And, yeah, Matt (the sommelier) wasn't here*
> *but they said these were from him,*
> *told us they were free!*
> *Well not free, they'd never use the f word,*
> *but that he "Wanted us to have them."*

asks for my glass back,

I hesitate.

I'm. a. quick. thinker.
but can't. work out.
how. to say.
I'm. not. finished.
yet.

I surrender my glass,
all my bubbles,
popped.

a simple welcome

a seeded bread roll drizzled in honey,
accompanied by a pot of cultured seaweed butter,
wedge of manchego, slices of iberico ham,
and a brine heavy drink

A Simple Welcome

bread with sesame and honey
manchego cheese with almond
thin sliced ham so fresh it shines
like cling film

shimmer burgundy
creamed with spanish fat
chestnut sweet

the smile of the waiter
the fire deglazing
she places the napkin on his lap
like he's a child

the butter's foamed
melted and ready
for the feast to begin

If That's Hello,
Goodbye Might Kill Me

The noir hit me so fast
I was halfway through
my inner monologue before
I realised what I was doing,

>*I knew she was trouble*
>*the moment she walked in*
>*all smooth leg, shaved nutmeg,*
>*unmistakable fishnet rind*
>*smelling of firm but gentle leather*
>*shouting, "Manchego, manchego,*
>*oh god please put me in your mouth*
>*and bite! But don't forget my flesh,*
>*candy cane sheen, iberico fat thighs,*
>*nurtured on nothing but acorns*
>*and free time. Then spend some*
>*attention on the sticky, seedy,*
>*lick-each-of-your-fingers-after-touching-me*
>*natural brown mound beneath*
>*before drowning in my olive grove brine,*
>*hint of lemon, kiss of garlic,*
>*mmm yes,*
>*know now,*
>*that you*
>*are mine."*

pebble

a plate covered in rocks,
two are dark chocolates
filled with foie gras,
choose wisely

As if Our Teeth Weren't Broken Enough

Eat shit or die.

If those are my only choices,

sure, I'll give it a try.

My Poems Are Like Pebbles

on a beach
battered by a life
that crashes
waves on the beach
in Jamaica
the morning after
my daddy
drunk
hits my mother
with the back of his hand
flow in out in out
like taking breath
after a panic attack
pick up the pebbles
examine them
when one catches your eye
a glint of quartz or hag stone
a hole you look through
to see ghosts
keep them
in your pocket
hold them
in your fist

.

washcloth

presented as a mint on slate
until watered, when it blooms
into an herb-scented washcloth

No One Said Magic
Had to Be Useful

I believe in magic
for the same reason
I am afraid of the dark;
you don't know
what you don't know
until after it has torn
your throat out.

So I found the mint
that grew into a washcloth
when watered, wildly
enchanting. Childlike,
I nearly clapped
when the rosemary oil
reached my nose.

Didn't care that
they'd laid a napkin
over my lap earlier,
that I'd already licked
my fingers fully clean,
or that any remnants
I wrapped in this white flag
to take with me would carry
with them the smell of defeat.
> *Not that I expected*
> *any scraps to survive*
> *when served such*
> *small plates.*

The Pill

    sits on black slate
white, perfect and round
the size of a Trebor mint.

      a pill sits on the hand, pale yellow
      flecked with deep down dirt, an escape
      from five days living in this room of boys
      their foetid smells, their mute violent lips.

i haven't eaten all day
saving myself for this feast
sticky finger bitten treat.

      we spent all our money on
      flavoured tobacco, cherry menthol
      three rollups in and i've gagged already.
      it's all we've got. it's better than going hungry.

an accompanying look of confusion
between us as the waiter lifts up the jug
sluices over the pill with water
scented with lemon and eucalyptus –
watch it grow into a white tower.

      it's five days since i got kicked out of home
      i've signed on the dole but no money for two weeks.
      no food to eat. just this pill. a present
      from a friend to cheer me up.
      i think fuck you mother
      before i take my first ecstacy tablet

proffered cloth to cleanse fingers
kissed by sesame, honey, nut fattened ham
dab dark chocolate and parfait rapture
from my upturned lips, cloth so hot it stings.

>*we talk continuously for three days*
>*before the darkness takes us,*
>*smoke our week's worth of tobacco,*
>*lit off the end of the ones we finish.*
>*no money for a shower token.*
>*16 years old and my voice rasps*
>*like an old woman's.*

the waiter leaves to bring another course.
we're relieved we didn't make fools of ourselves.
eating the napkins, eating the knives.

lamb

lamb tartare with salsa verde,
hidden by nasturtium leaves,
and green tea powder

Spirited Away // No-Face

Some spirit
scooped this flesh
fresh from the earth
placed the mini Miyazaki
forest onto my rough
edged plate,
dark fluid oozing out
one side while the other
remains still dust dry
from a shower
of matcha powder.
in the middle, tropaeolum trees scattered
like upside down frog's umbrellas
make me feel like a child

> *And not just because our server*
> *slowly folded my napkin carefully*
> *over my groin without a hint of*
> *interest or hesitation.*
> *it's deeper, feels like living*
> *out of Florida motels again, waiting*
> *for Toonami to steal me away*
> *two precious hours each day.*

I take a bite to find sharp
salsa verde coating
chewy cubes that
I can only describe
as meat gummies

and just like that
I am no longer Nausicaa,
cannot consider myself
Mononoke Hime,
and stooping to lick
the plate, I see I am
not even Sōsuke,
only Greed.

Gush

in from the fields / scalpel knife intersects / raw
and bleeding / you cry for your mother / reflex
spills milk from her teats / white stars in white
wool / before the pool / red gush of blood from
your throat / red wine cool / white wine warm /
mixed with your jus / the spice balanced
against the soft / the meat / nestled in green
chilli / eyes clouds / roll to white

ragstone

a hot and cold leafless salad,
goat's cheese, brown onion foam,
candied walnuts

Ragstone

you grow hungry   appetite inflamed
the stone bowl   waiting   warm

to the touch   the spoon   hesitates
sits   for a moment   before digging

the brown foam   hides   its gold
goat cheese treasure   cool   sticky

in the warm mousse   you savour
this simple course   its eye watering

cost   the foam rich   the candied
walnuts break   under the crush

of teeth   hardened   with mercury
against   the grind   against

the poverty   weakened   by three
sugars in every tea to fight the pangs

the cost of   weekly shop   expands
electricity price rises   gas

builds up   held firm   in the foam
the mousse sets   each tiny course

                    fills you up slowly

Something Taller Than Everest

Growing up I only saw it
in my free school meals;
a few torn sheets of wilted
iceberg, stiff cabbage slices,
and unripe cherry tomatoes
with a penchant for popping
messily, seed stains stayed
stalwart through the next
few wears of that shirt,
laundry a land rarely visited.

Later I sought salads out myself,
spent half the food budget
overcompensating for my youth.
Learned to pepper steady
streams of leafy greens
with bits of apple, blue cheese,
and raspberry vinaigrette.

But when I met this
hot/cold goat's cheese
cream, candied walnut
crunch, self-contradictory
burnt-onion powder
leafless construction
it was obvious,
I hadn't explored far enough.

rabbit

a chinese style dumpling
seasoned with tarragon,
dashi, rabbit, and eel

The Cyclical Nature of Sestina and Trauma

the course comes out - a small haunch of rabbit,
a dumpling with dashi, eel, and smoke.
i revel in the flavours, the odd sensations,
the drunkenness, the weight of the evening,
the addition of tarragon, the dark stone bowl.
the preparation for writing my trauma.

it's not easy to do - to write this trauma
thinking back to the times i was a frightened rabbit.
ink and water incantation, hand waved over a bowl
peer through twenty years, through memory smoke.
seek out the nuance, reach back to an evening,
dry-mouthed, feel this uncomfortable sensation.

the fear. how do you write this sensation?
the homeless hostel. unpick *that* trauma.
John Peel on the radio, 11pm in the evening.
he's playing a new band, Frightened Rabbit.
the single bed where we sit, roll spliffs, smoke
ourselves stupid. he packs the bowl.

take another hit. this forty year old man is no dish,
no beautiful man to fill me with the sensations
i want late into the night. met him in the smoking
area outside a club. now he's on my bed. the trauma
in writing this moment catches me now. timid rabbit.
thinking back to this particular evening.

i met him at a psychedelic rave late evening
in summer. 16 years old. addicted to pot,
to speed, to whatever i could. a Duracell bunny
always on the go because *what if I stopped*? no sense
at 16. i played with whoever i pleased. the trauma
of my mother's house catching up, burnt

out but carrying on, meeting men like twisting fire.
the single bed in the hostel. have him over on an evening
kiss it. hold it. do it in the dark. hide the trauma.
he can't see the cuts. life in this leaking goldfish bowl -
i'm swimming round and round, the sensation
spilling, smashing into walls. the man tells me to rub it.

Why Wasn't This Served With Three Fingers of Laphroaig?

When it touched my tongue
I tasted appropriation,
        tarragon and dashi?
like pornography
taboo's hard to define
until rabbit and eel
are covered in
each others juices
a cultural looseness
familiar to the French
perhaps, but unthinkable
for Japanese society
where hare is like dog,
it doesn't belong
on a plate.

But, being
poor/American/immigrant
I smiled, revelled in the excess
and saved my shame
to digest alone, later.

mussels

mussels and pork fat croutons
covered in hollandaise sauce,
powdered seaweed, and coal oil

Mussels With Coal Oil

mussels in a hollandaise sauce
with coal oil, pork fat croutons,
dashi

mussels   sit squat   in the dark bowl
squat   in the throat   squat
in pale yellow   meadow green

the addition of coal oil gives the dish
an unusual robust flavour

the addition   of coal oil   gives the family
rough heritage   dirty hands   mucky faces
lungs   that cough
             black lacework

during the late 19th and most
of the 20th century Armthorpe was known
for its coal mining; the pit Markham Main

the village rises   men kiss their sleepy wives
over the tea kettle   look in   on the children
tossing in bed   leave the house   pass
fields of lowing cows   in the dawn light

during the miners' strike only 34 of Armthorpe's
1300 miners went back to work

the excavation   work   is backbreaking
men with legs   like tree trunks
roots   in the earth   roots
in the village   muscles tight   and taut
                              ache at night

when they retire   these giants   turn human
shrinking   under the bright sunlight

> three people from the village of Armthorpe
> have died of VCJD, the human form
> of mad cow disease, two who lived
> on the same street

i'm 11   after opening our presents
we visit   my grandparents   my uncle
lays on a single bed   in the front room
by the christmas tree   lit up like a rainbow
        curtains wide open

        he can't eat

but   screams

  the   whole   way   through

   our family's christmas dinner

     his cracker   sits unopened

the third victim, Adrian Hodgkinson, 24,
lived in Harrogate, dying in 1997
he spent every weekend between 1972
and 1986 at his grandmother's house
in Armthorpe eating Sunday dinner

for the last few months   of my uncle's life
he couldn't walk
his muscles

       wasted

away

hake

a morsel of white fish,
a series of sliced heritage carrots,
amd an orange sauce

John D. Rockefeller

This was unfamiliar.
I could tell it was white,
end of conversation.
I've seen food like this,
but not often enough
to intuit whether it's
cod or haddock or...

>   *Hake? Okay,*
>   *if you say so.*

When I look it up later
It turns out there are
thirteen distinct species
of this fish but no notes
on whether the flavour
wavers between them,
nothing about what
makes them unique,
just talk of where they
came from.

This,
this is very familiar,
I can tell, it is white
and rich.

I Drink at Least Two Litres
of Water Every Day

i wonder
when it went soft
bendy
the skin faded
to a pale wrinkled
white rind

ancient carrots
were purple
until bred
samizdat orange
one thickness
each a facsimile

i look in the mirror
my body soft
my body flaccid
in bright sunshine

yellow light
reflected onto breasts
that droop
a back that creaks
crepe paper
secret smile

they say
if you put a carrot
leaf side down
in water
they'll perk back up

On the Pinot

when I joked the wine looked like Ribena, watery
at the edges, the waiter looked at me like I was
see-through. she joked the other one looked like
Fanta - I mean - it did. But there's something
in it, something out of it, a fish splashing on the
pavement. Maybe I'm imagining it. All our talk
of race and judgement and class and trauma and
I'm swept up looking for

every

single

slight

bbq

*a bite of boneless short rib
served with beetroot bbq sauce,
pickled onion, maldon sea salt,
and wicked bumblebee switchblade*

Jus the Colour of Canned Cranberries, My Only Food When Homeless

Two tiny bites
of beef
bleeding
beet juice
barbecue
trick switchblade
bee-stings
through
short rib
topped by
softly
saurkrauted
onion slice
sprinkled
simply
with maldon
sea salt for a
satisfying crunch
of resistance
like my own bones
crushed by the jaws
of giants, smiling
so wide,
always
hungry.

The Roast Beef of Old England

beef
   for the gentleman
     beef   for
      aristocrats
        beef
      milk and cream

[we fed them to each other]
  making
       the animals   tough and
                vulnerable
          nourished and fattened
       until slaughter

bathroom break

even us poors,
have to keep some secrets

Like a Virgin

the toilet paper is tucked
into a neat little triangle
the first time I go
to the bathroom

I must be the first one in

the toilet paper is tucked
into a neat little triangle
the second time I go
to the bathroom

a painted
little
strumpet

fondue

a pot of baked french cheese
served with caramelised onions
and bread for dipping

Fondue Four Nights a Week Without Cheese

If I ever had a teddy bear
it was lost to Dad's murder
or Mom's vices long before
the flames came for my things.
Instead, I spent my nights
trying to sleep away
pre-pubescent hunger, fleeing
from empty-stomach pain
only to wake and split
a loaf of cheap bread.
Angel and I dealt with this
differently, my method
always to compress;
carefully pepper
with immense pressure
slowly roll into a ball
until thick, dense,
smile after every bite
almost convinced
it was real
food.

rhubarb fool

a traditional fool made with rhubarb,
topped with a trio of chocolates,
served in a granite cube

Gretel

at the back of the garden under the apple tree
where gnarling branches finger fat poison fruit,
the hum of summer bees collect rose-scented
pollen, witch-tricked in sweetness. small hands
gathered the flush of rhubarb, maiden pink with
shame, snapped off, leaf-whipped for immersion
in crumble and custard, cinnamon for seasoning,
sugar to make the stem sweet, sugar to make the
children sweet, butter to grease them like fat little
pigs, slipping out of the grasp of the giant. sunday
lunch with gravy and puddings and then comes
dessert. *fee fi fo fum* I smell the blood of an english
woman, locked in the bathroom, hiding from the
post sunday roast wrath, the *old peculiar*-fueled
yorkshireman snarling, echoing the roar of the
engines of the telly as me and my sister turn up
the volume of the formula one while the crumble
blackens in the oven

Rhubarb Fools

Rhubarb is forced,
grows up so fast.
Hear his body break.

Our youths were
never meant to be
spent this quickly.

But we were born
in darkness,
our light, a lie.

chocolate

a series of brown squares
of varying textures, thicknesses,
and deconstructed cuba libre flavours

Chocolate

as sweet as this is,
there's something
unsavoury in the
flavour that gets left
in my mouth when
i know the people
who serve this food
don't get to eat
like this. i spit the
cuba libre inspired
dessert into my
thick cloth napkin.

Taste Buds Always Tell
the Bitter Truth

Mondrian sees the city
only from above
in hermetically
sealed squares.
Tiny, tidy,
neatly nested
next to, never
overlapping.

In his gaze
nothing is
out of place,
the populace fits
precisely into their
prescribed boxes,
happy, well fed,
safe, content.

In his hangings
the lie stands
like Steve Cohen
in a three piece suit
looking down on us
through panoramic
penthouse views.

But from down here,
sleeping-on-the-streets level,
the city's sins are painted shades

of cuba libre brown, every dirty thought
swept under too-thin chocolate sheets,
cola gummies exchanged like money,
buys access to bodies odorous and wet
bite, cum, shudder, lick stale sweat
bury us under lime zest.

We are placed on plates,
appearing picture perfect
and they call us dessert.

cloud

a gin and lemon cloud,
served on a silver spoon

Like Your Last Dollar
a Week After Payday

A single spoonful of eggy,
lemon-scented gin cloud
briefly tickles my tongue
        – Suddenly!
The meal is done.
        Is that it?

You Don't Belong Here

egg white / gin kiss / trout lip
spoon tip / for the final
/ cheap trick

i could have bought
a month's worth of food
for a family of three

for just one night in this
fire-lit boudoir

pints in the pub after

a crisp, aromatic pale ale with
clean and refreshing citrus-fruit flavours

Last Orders

pulling pints or partners
at the local after work
where folks speak freely -
this is what saves some of us

> *wapentake - an assembly or meeting place,*
> *at a crossroads or near a river, one's vote*
> *was taken by a show of weapons*

in the pub, chat through the feast we enjoyed
hypothesise how to remake nearly-michelin-starred
courses in our own kitchens - beetroot bbq sauce,
the power of rabbit, eel, tarragon and dashi

> *japanese broth - simmer and slurp*
> *take things out of the sea*
> *taking the sea out of them*

there's poverty here -
the poor drink small beer
eat seaweed and leftovers
buy each other drinks based
on who got paid most recently

> *the 1854 cholera outbreak - doctor snow*
> *realises those who don't get sick are drinking*
> *so much beer that they aren't drinking water*

for the smiths beer was water
reached for first to quench thirst,
barely recognised for the buzz
it brings, a kiss in comparison
to opioid bee stings.

hogarth's beer street and gin lane, 1751 –
contrasted the health and productivity benefits
of drinking beer with the vice of gin drinking

at seven years old, I learn drinking
isn't all it's cracked up to be –
daddy's handprint painted red
across mummy's cheek

head quickly swells with stout's firm body
texas gold fills the glass – drink this
medicine, wash away the taste of defeat

sit alone in the corner of the bar
head down, stare into the murk
left where spilled beer coalesces
mouth like gunfire until leon notices,
brings you into the cheer of idle chatter

you don't become a regular until you have
drunk in the same pub for at least 10 years,
spending over 1/3 of your income throughout

being a regular is its own brand of joy
fresh pint sat waiting when you arrive
the in-joke and smile shared with the girl
behind the bar – yeah, we're the same

more than 80% of women said yes,
they had experienced sexual harassment
while working in a pub or bar

this one grabs your tits, grins and gurns,
you raise your fist, a clear shot to the eye,
red and black once you pull back

one in four britons will meet
their future marriage partner
in the arms of a local pub

this one's tall, dark, and surly
but he knows your drink order
and three summers later you make
your vows on bow bridge in central park

the blood-lust of goddess sekhmet sated
only by red beer she mistook for blood - suddenly
so drunk she gives up the slaughter altogether

three swords, baby faced assassin,
cannonball, heart and soul, transmission,
raspberry summer shock of sam smith's

and they asked me in to dinner,
to get the beauty of it hot—
HURRY UP PLEASE IT'S TIME

HURRY UP PLEASE IT'S TIME
goonight bill. goonight lou. goonight may.
goonight. ta ta. goonight. goonight.

LAST ORDERS AT THE BAR PLEASE!
we spill out, laughing, into blustery snow
wrapped in warm light and old jokes,
new number on a napkin in your pocket.

Poem Authors

Apparently She Was Just Helping Us to Our Table	CC
A Simple Welcome	JH
If That's Hello, Goodbye Might Kill Me	CC
As if Our Teeth Weren't Broken Enough	CC
My Poems Are Like Pebbles	JH
No One Said Magic Had to Be Useful	CC
The Pill	JH
Spirited Away // No-Face	CC
Gush	JH
Ragstone	JH
Something Taller Than Everest	CC
The Cyclical Nature of Sestina and Trauma	JH
Why Wasn't This Served With Three Fingers of Laphroaig?	CC
Mussels With Coal Oil	JH
John D. Rockefeller	CC
I Drink at Least Two Litres of Water Every Day	JH
On the Pinot	JH
Jus the Colour of Canned Cranberries, My Only Food [...]	CC
The Roast Beef of Old England	JH
Like a Virgin	JH
Fondue Four Nights a Week Without Cheese	CC
Gretel	JH
Rhubarb Fools	CC
Chocolate	JH
Taste Buds Always Tell the Bitter Truth	CC
Like Your Last Dollar a Week After Payday	CC
You Don't Belong Here	JH
Last Orders	JH & CC

Acknowledgements

'Last Orders' was a commissioned poem, first published by *Women on Tap* 2022.

'Mussels' first appeared in *Anthropocene*, 2022.

'Rabbit' appeared in *Anti Heroin Chic*, 2022.

'gretel' was published in *an othered mother, (Nine Pens Press*, 2022).

LAY OUT YOUR UNREST